Since 1066 every English monarch, except Edwards V and VIII, has been crowned in Westminster Abbey (*inset above*). Many are also buried here, sharing their resting place with other famous people – poets, scientists, politicians and soldiers, including the Unknown Warrior.

The Victorian–Gothic building of the Houses of Parliament (*above*) is the centre of British government. The best view is from Albert Embankment, with Victoria Tower at one end and the Clock Tower (called 'Big Ben' after its bell) at the other. A flag on the Victoria Tower by day, and a light in the Clock Tower (*right*) at night, shows that the House of Commons is sitting.

The ornate Gothic structure of the Albert Memorial (*left*) was funded by the public and parliament as a tribute to Queen Victoria's consort, and completed in 1876. The base and canopy rise to 175ft/53m and the bronze statue of Albert, holding a catalogue of the Great Exhibition, is 14ft/4m high.

Originally intended as a Hall of Arts and Sciences, Queen Victoria added the 'Royal Albert' when she laid the foundation stone in 1868. Now seen as another memorial to Prince Albert the oval amphitheatre (*right*), topped with a glass dome, stages many musical and sporting events, most notably the Promenade Concerts. The poor acoustics were greatly improved in 1968 by putting huge 'saucers' in the dome.

Its fine collection of buildings including Wren's Royal Naval College (*inset right*), and old royal park, make Greenwich a very popular choice for day trips. The National Maritime Museum (*right*) was founded in 1934 and is the largest of its kind in the world. Flamsteed House and the Old Royal Observatory are also part of the Museum. The famous Greenwich Meridian is in the Observatory Courtyard so you can stand in the eastern and western hemispheres at the same time.

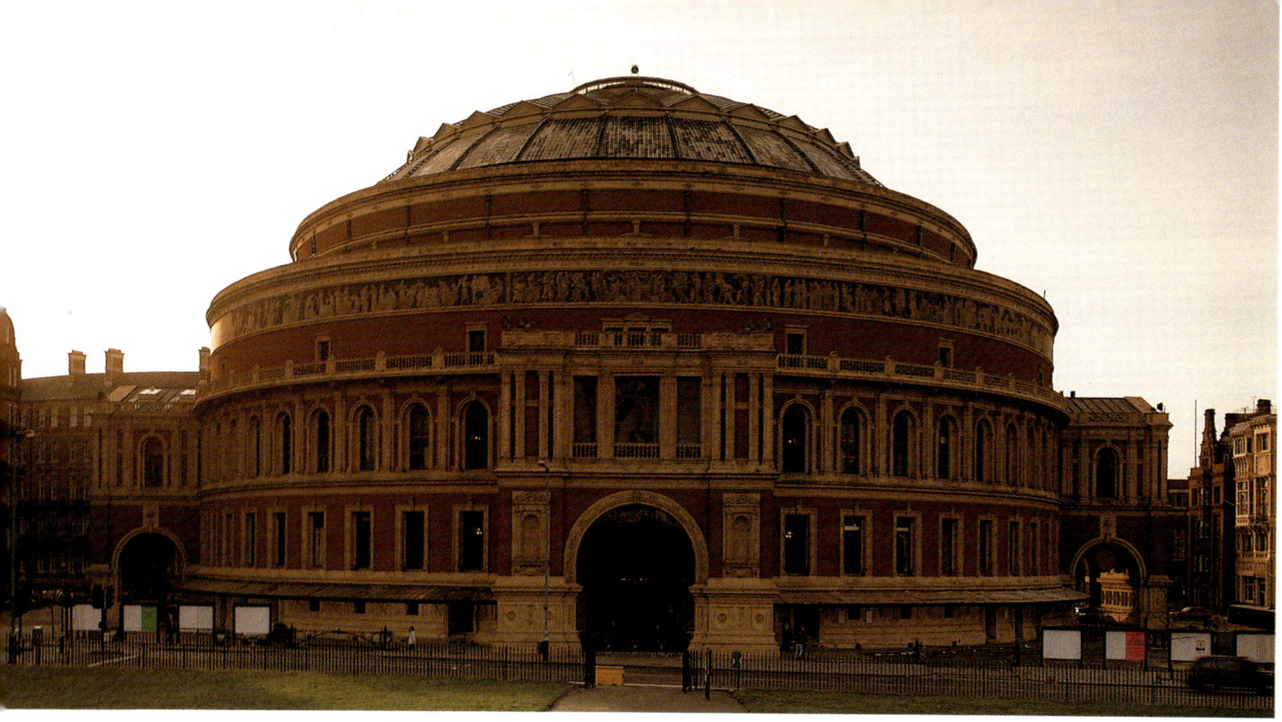

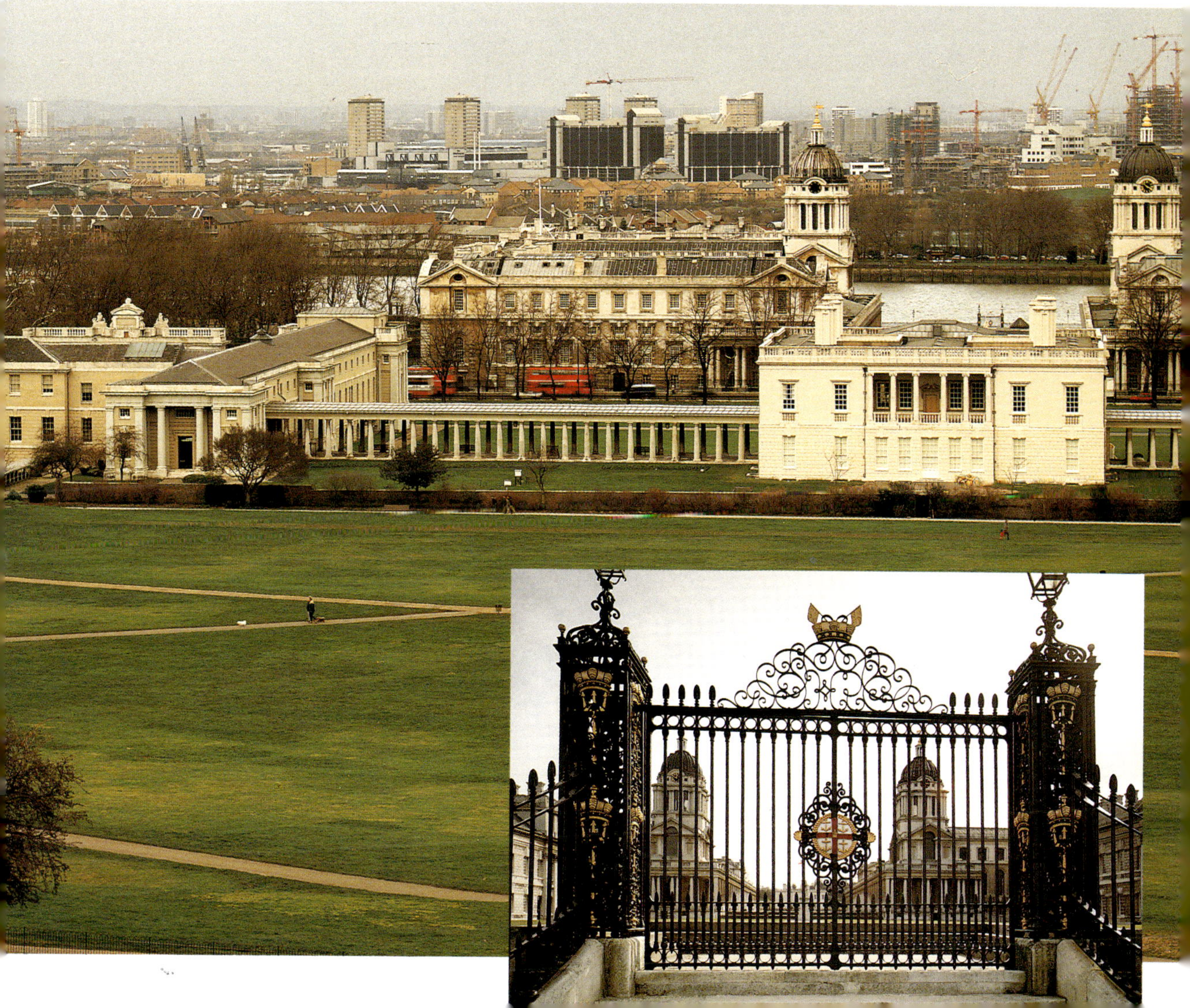

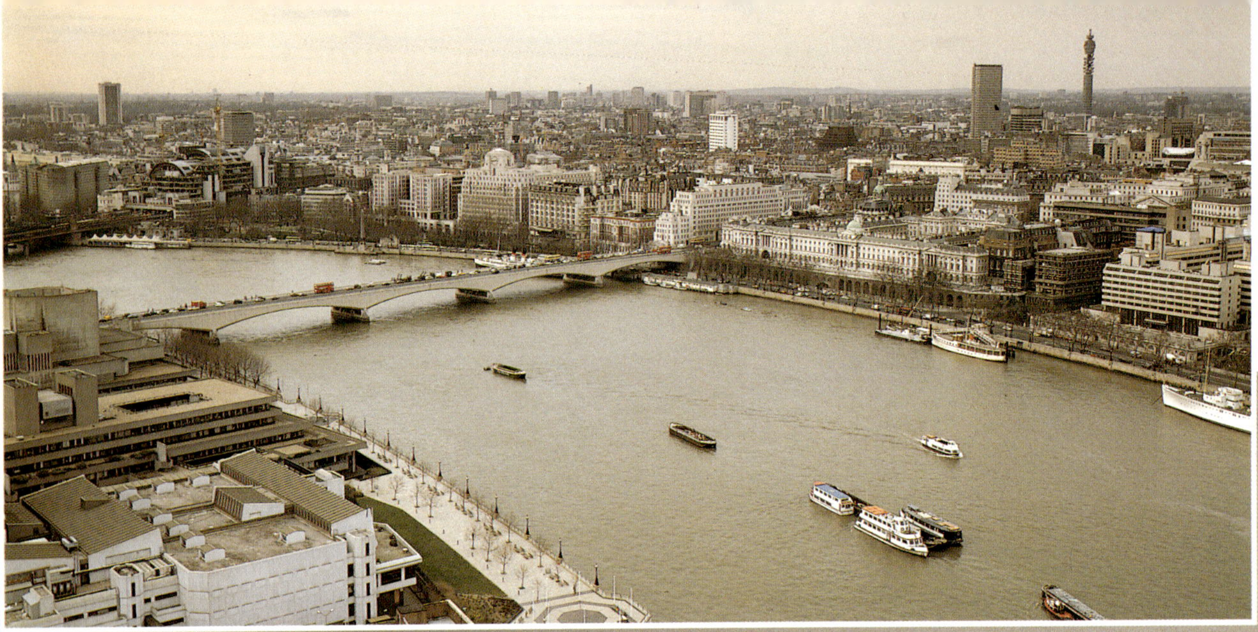
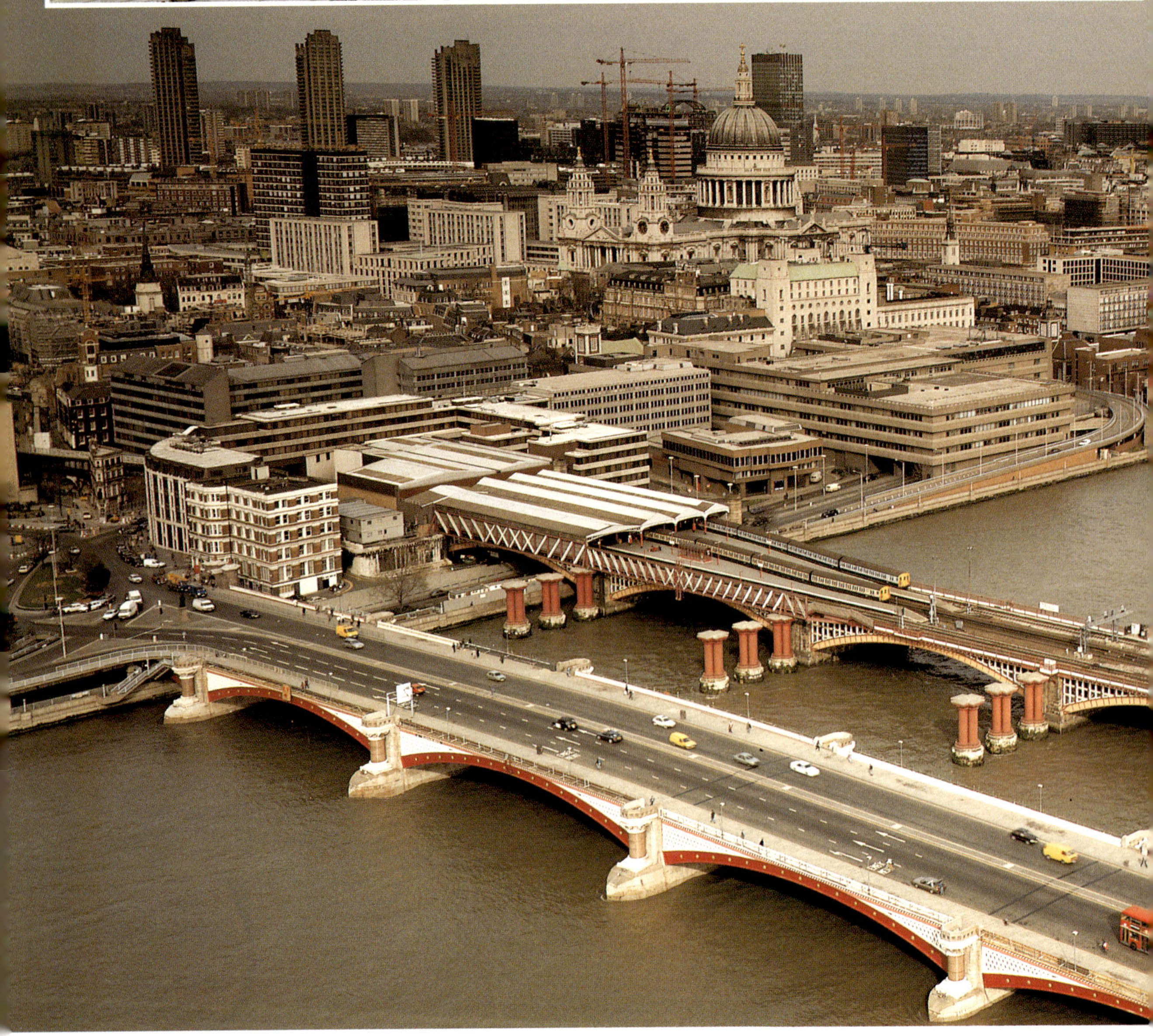

The impressive London skyline to the east (*below*) contrasts the Baroque splendour of St Paul's, and other Wren churches, with the many skyscrapers of modern London, including the National Westminster Tower, Britain's tallest building.

Looking west (*left*) the countryside of the Home Counties can be seen in the distance, while the distinctive Telecom Tower rises sharply nearer the centre of London.

Wren's Monument (*right*), 202ft/62m high, commemorates the Great Fire which broke out 202ft/62m away in Pudding Lane. Climb the 311 steps for a marvellous view.

Buckingham Palace (*above*) was made official London residence of the Sovereign by Queen Victoria. The Royal Standard flies when the Queen is in residence but you're unlikely to see her unless an important occasion, such as a royal wedding, brings the family out onto the famous first-floor balcony.

St James's Palace (*left and above left*) was built by Henry VIII but did not become the principal royal residence until the end of the 17thC. Although Queen Victoria moved the court to Buckingham Palace, foreign ambassadors are still accredited to the Court of St James before being received at Buckingham Palace.

William and Mary were the first royals to live in Kensington Palace (*right*), an unpretentious red-brick building where the Prince and Princess of Wales and Princess Margaret now have apartments. Queen Victoria, whose statue, by her daughter Princess Louise, stands outside, was born here.

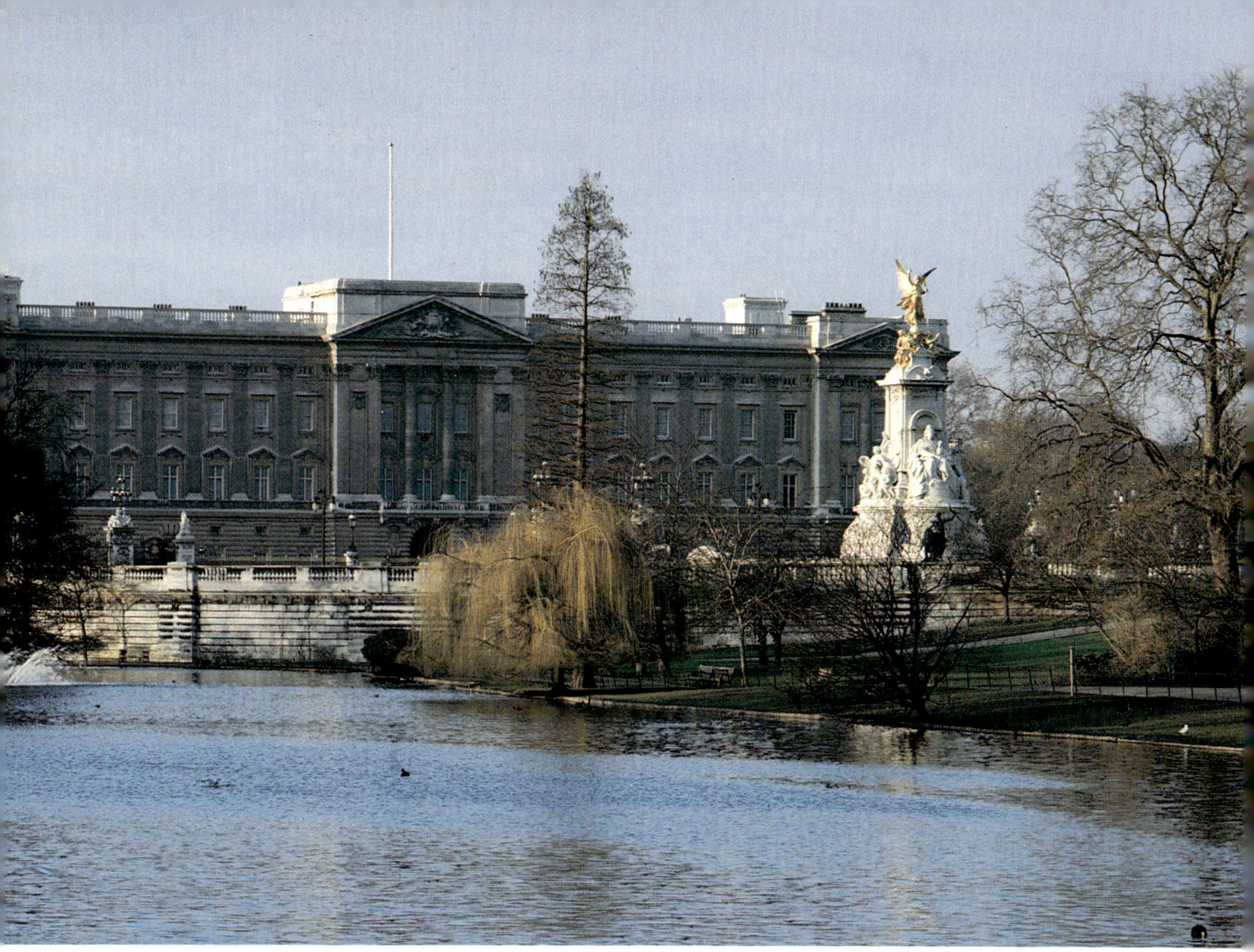

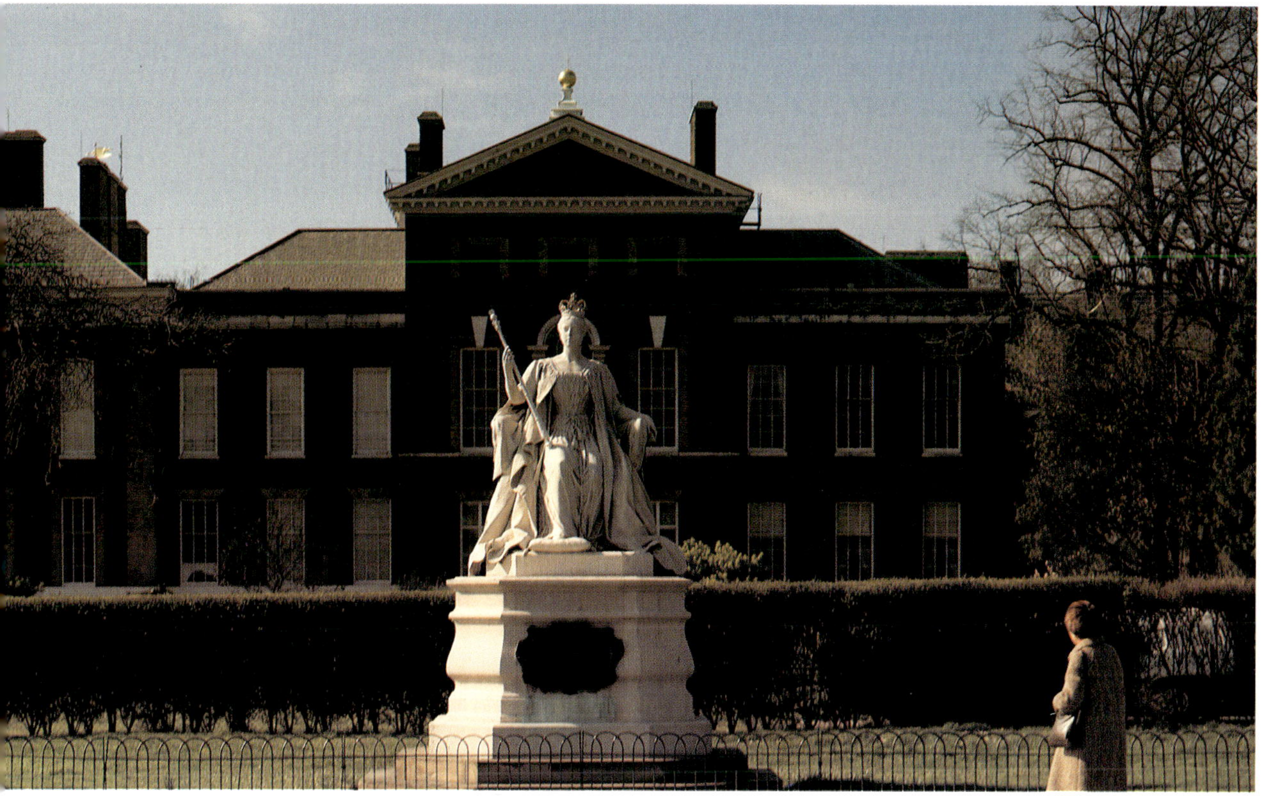

Hampton Court (*right*) is a splendid palace on the Thames, combining fine Tudor architecture with graceful additions by Wren. Famous for the Great Vine, the Maze, the Astronomical Clock, the Great Hall and the Grace and Favour lodgings for Crown pensioners (first provided by George III). The oldest part of the Tower of London is the White Tower (*below*) begun by William the Conqueror. London's oldest royal residence has served as palace, prison and fortress, and now houses the Crown Jewels and the Royal Armouries. Perhaps most famous as a prison and for its many ill-fated occupants (including Anne Boleyn) who were executed here, the Tower holds a grim fascination for its many visitors.

Windsor Castle (*below right*) owes much of its present appearance to George IV (reigned 1820–30) although there has been a fortress on the site since 1080: which makes Windsor the oldest royal residence. The most famous attractions today are Henry II's Round Tower, Queen Mary's Dolls' House and St George's Chapel – where the annual Garter Service is held in June.

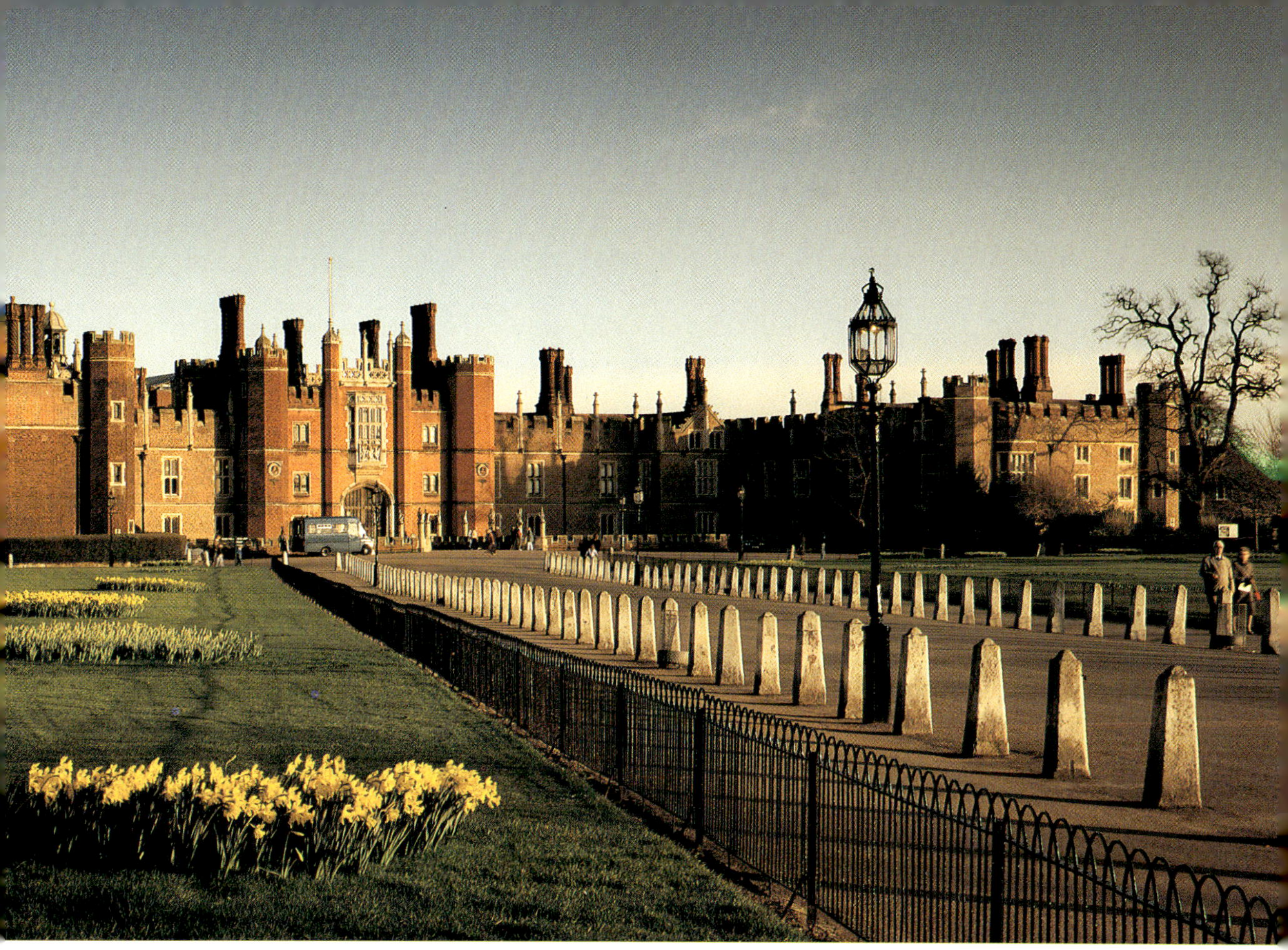

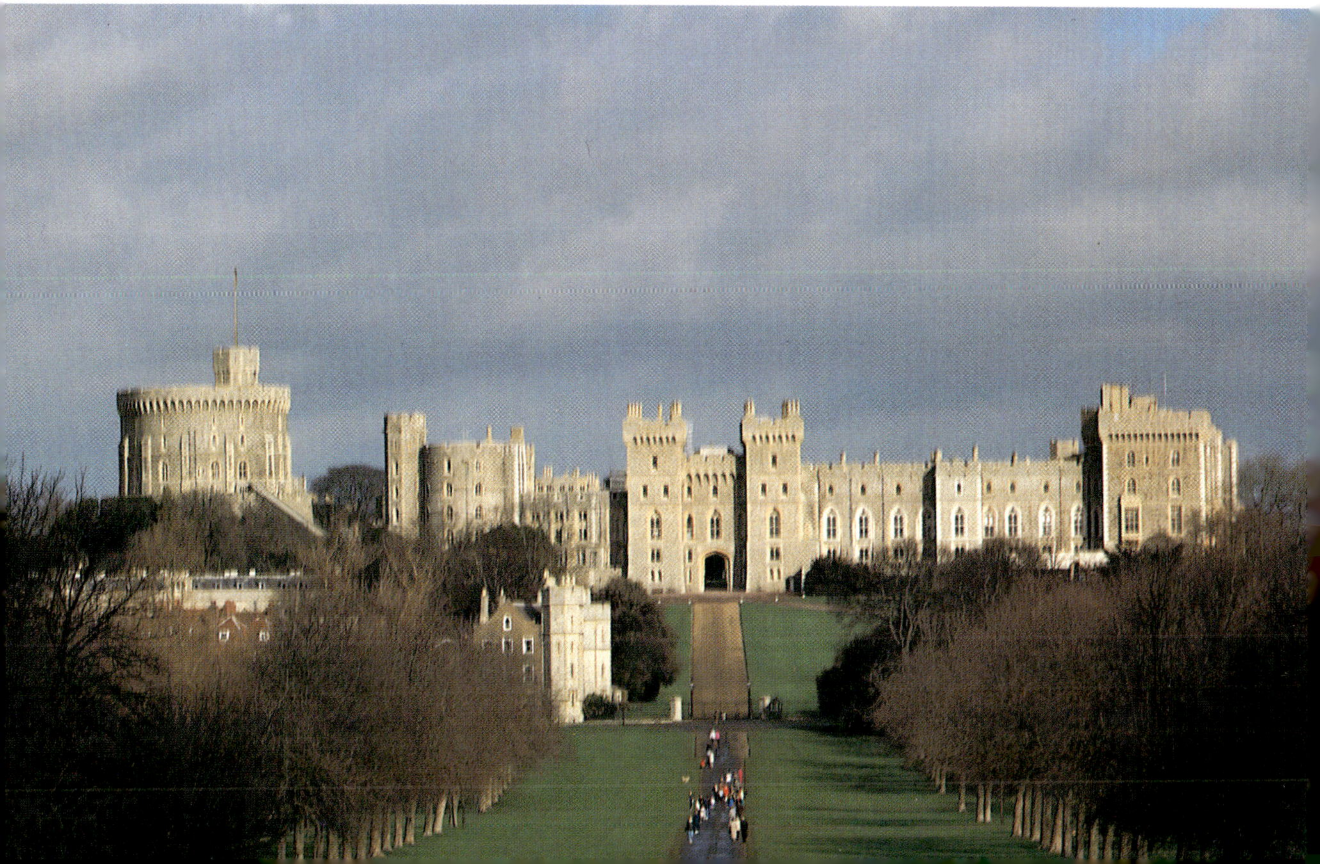

Lloyds of London (*far left*) is a world-famous international insurance market. The 12-storey dealing room is housed in a 246ft/75m-high glass-roofed atrium surrounded by galleries and service towers. The whole hi-tech structure, built 1981–86, is linked by glass-sided escalators and external glass-sided lifts.

The Guildhall (*left*) dates from 1411, though it was severely damaged in the Great Fire and World War II. It hosts the annual Lord Mayor's Banquet and boasts the largest medieval crypt in London, a splendid Great Hall, a fine Library and a Clock Museum.

The high-rise buildings and modern offices of international business and finance stand out clearly against the skyline but the City of London (*below*), one of the world's leading financial centres, has always had a high proportion of other, more spiritual, dwellings, notably St Paul's.

Wren's English–Baroque masterpiece, St Paul's (*right and below right*), was built 1675–1710. The great dome, 112ft/34m in diameter, dominates the City and the London skyline. It stands 365ft/111m high and is the second largest dome in the world after St Peter's, Rome. The view from the Golden Gallery at the top is spectacular.

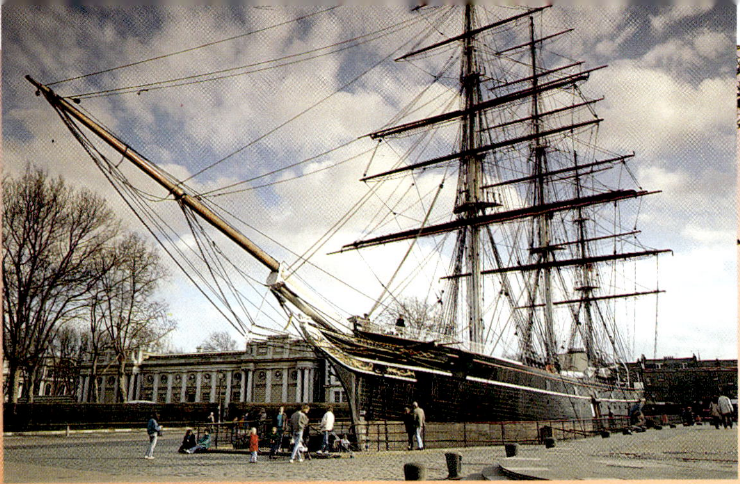

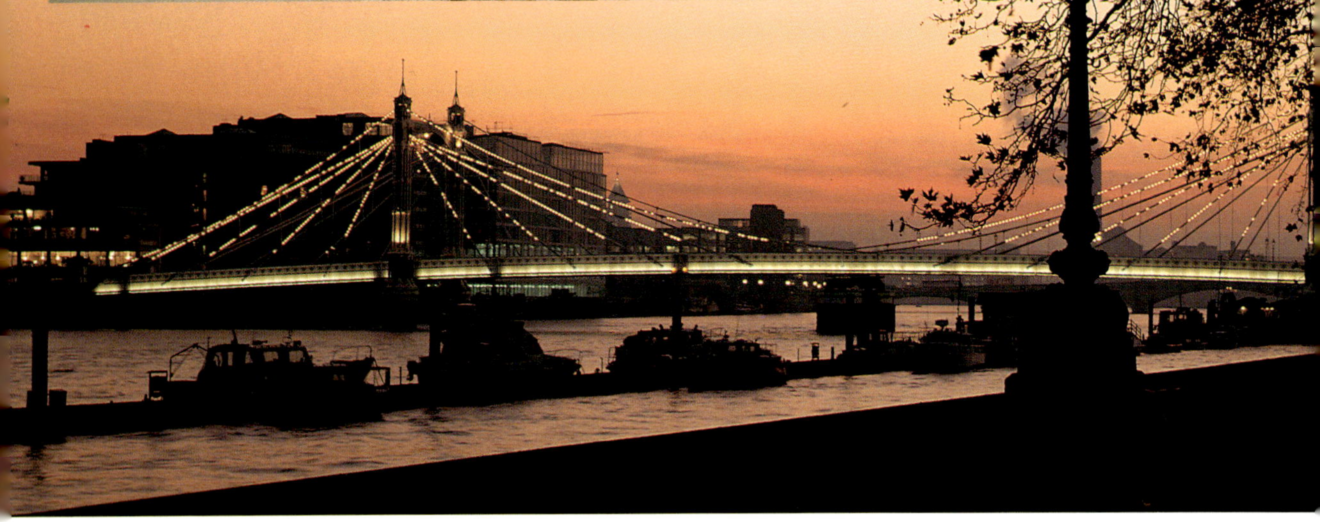

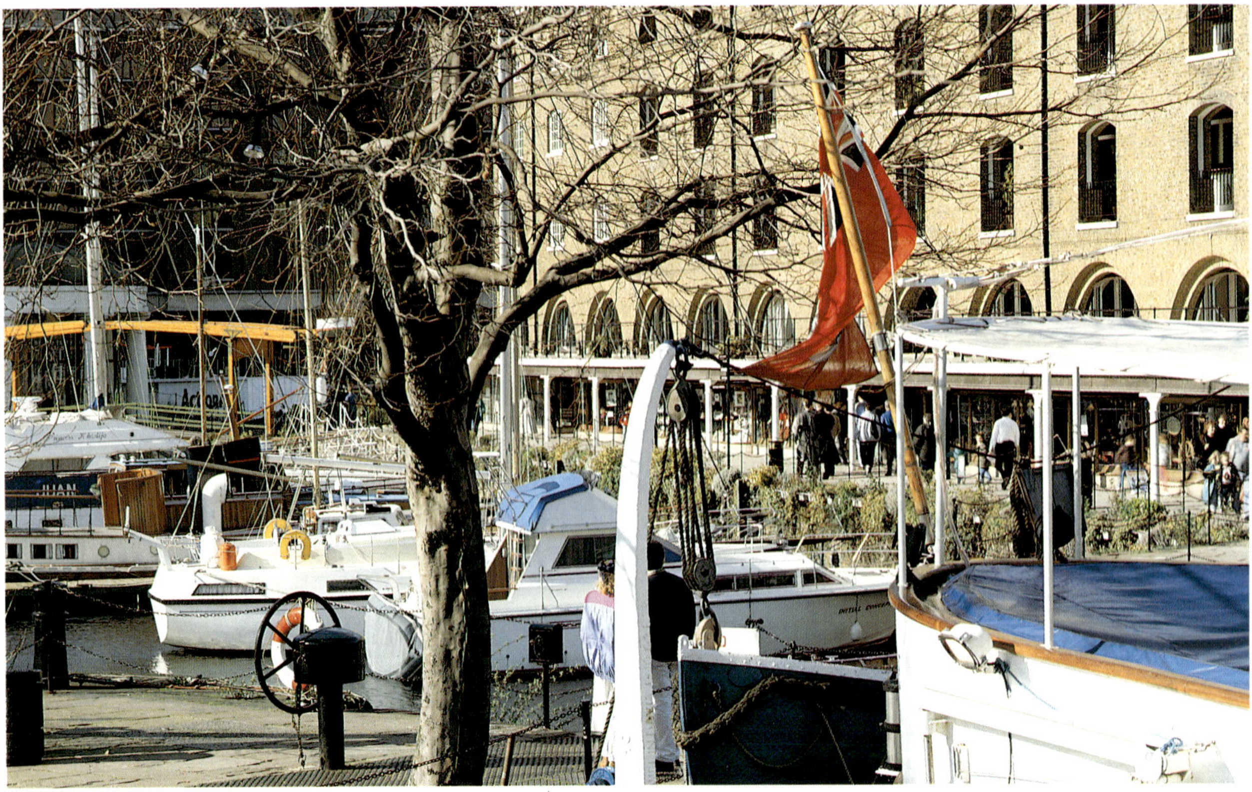

The elegant *Cutty Sark* (*inset left*), last and fastest of the Victorian tea clippers, is now in permanent dry dock beside the Royal Naval College, Greenwich. On board there is a fascinating collection of photographs and figure heads, and moored nearby is Sir Francis Chichester's yacht, *Gipsy Moth IV*, in which he sailed single-handed around the world. Particularly attractive when illuminated, the Albert Bridge (*left*) is a combination of cantilever and suspension and was built by Ordish, 1871–73. It links Chelsea Embankment on the north bank with Battersea on the south. St Katharine's Dock (*below left*) ceased operating commercially in 1968. It is now a business centre and yacht haven where modern buildings like the Tower Hotel and the World Trade Centre contrast with the restored Ivory House – a 19thC warehouse – home to apartments, offices and shops. As well as private yachts, the steam tug *Challenge*, the Nore lightship, and several large and distinctive Thames barges are berthed here. The Victorian–Gothic Tower Bridge (*below*), designed by Horace Jones and John Wolfe-Barry, was opened in 1894. It is the most easterly bridge on the Thames and one of the world's best-known bascule bridges, which still opens to allow tall ships to pass through. There are wonderful views from the walkway and an interesting museum within the towers on the history, design and operation of this famous Thames landmark.

The National Gallery (*above*) was founded in 1824 and shows a representative selection of great paintings from the European schools.

The Royal Opera House (*below*) is home to the Royal Opera and the Royal Ballet. Most famous international stars perform here.

The British Museum (*top left*) is one of the largest museums in the world. Its galleries display Egyptian, Greek, Roman, Western Asiatic and British antiquities.

The Victorian-Romanesque Natural History Museum (*above right*) is home to the popular dinosaur exhibits.

The Theatre Museum (*inset*) traces the history of the English stage from the 17thC.

The South Bank Centre (*left*) is a huge arts complex.

Every Christmas there is a splendid tree in Trafalgar Square and festive lights in many London shopping streets. Whatever the design – snowmen, reindeer, Santas or colourful Christmas trees – Regent Street (*above left*) is a particularly sparkling sight. The Changing of the Guard (*above right*) takes place every day in summer and alternate days in winter at 11am in Whitehall and 11.30am outside Buckingham Palace. Guard mounting also takes place at St James's Palace, the Tower of London and Windsor Castle.

No ceremonial occasion would be complete without one or more of the State Coaches. Queen Alexandra's Coach (*below*) is used for State Visits and Royal Weddings as well as to convey the crown at the State Opening of Parliament.

The famous and colourful spectacle of the Trooping of the Colour (*below and left*) takes place each June in honour of the Queen's official birthday. Her Majesty rides in an open carriage from Buckingham Palace to the huge parade ground behind Horse Guards where she takes the Royal Salute at 11am. The Colour (flag) of one of the seven regiments of the Household Division is inspected and the Queen then reviews the Guards as they march to the music of massed bands. After returning to Buckingham Palace she appears on the balcony, with other members of the royal family, to view the RAF fly-past at 1pm.

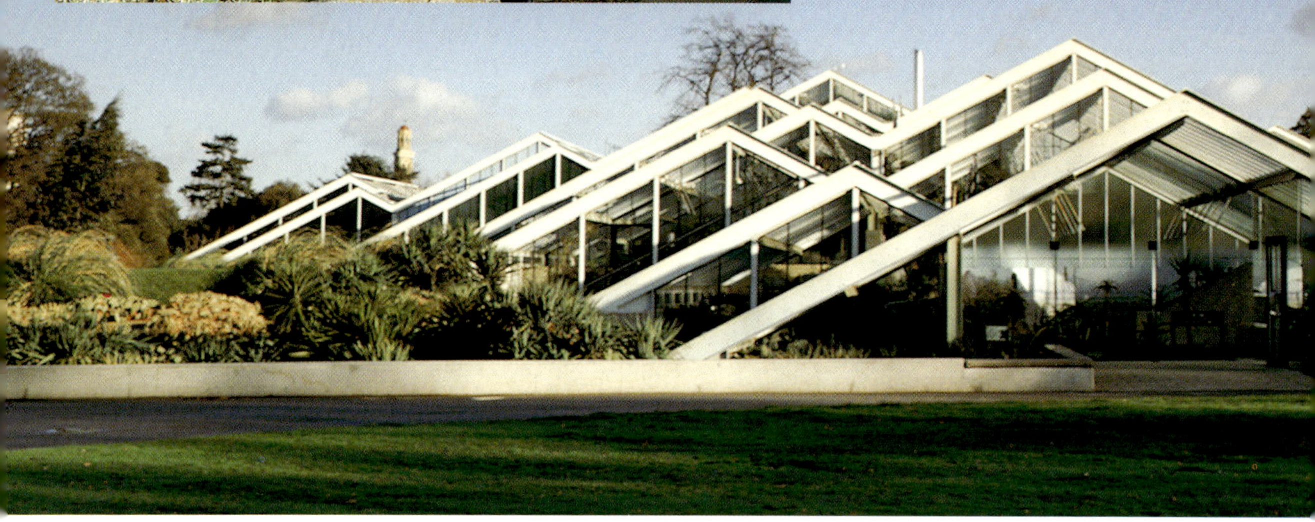

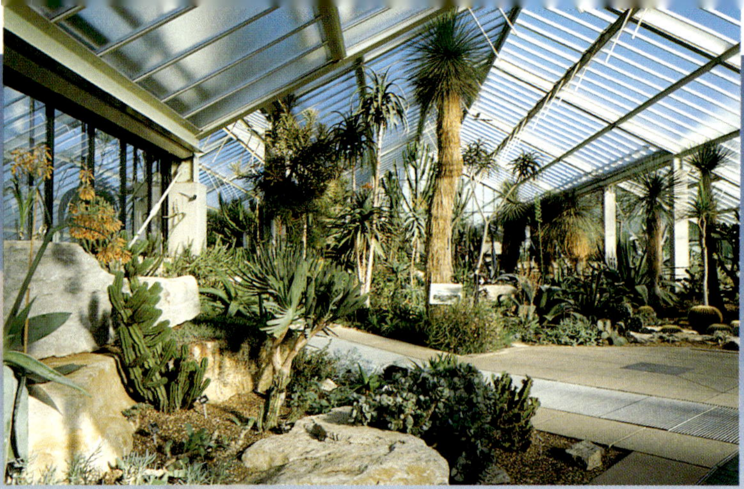

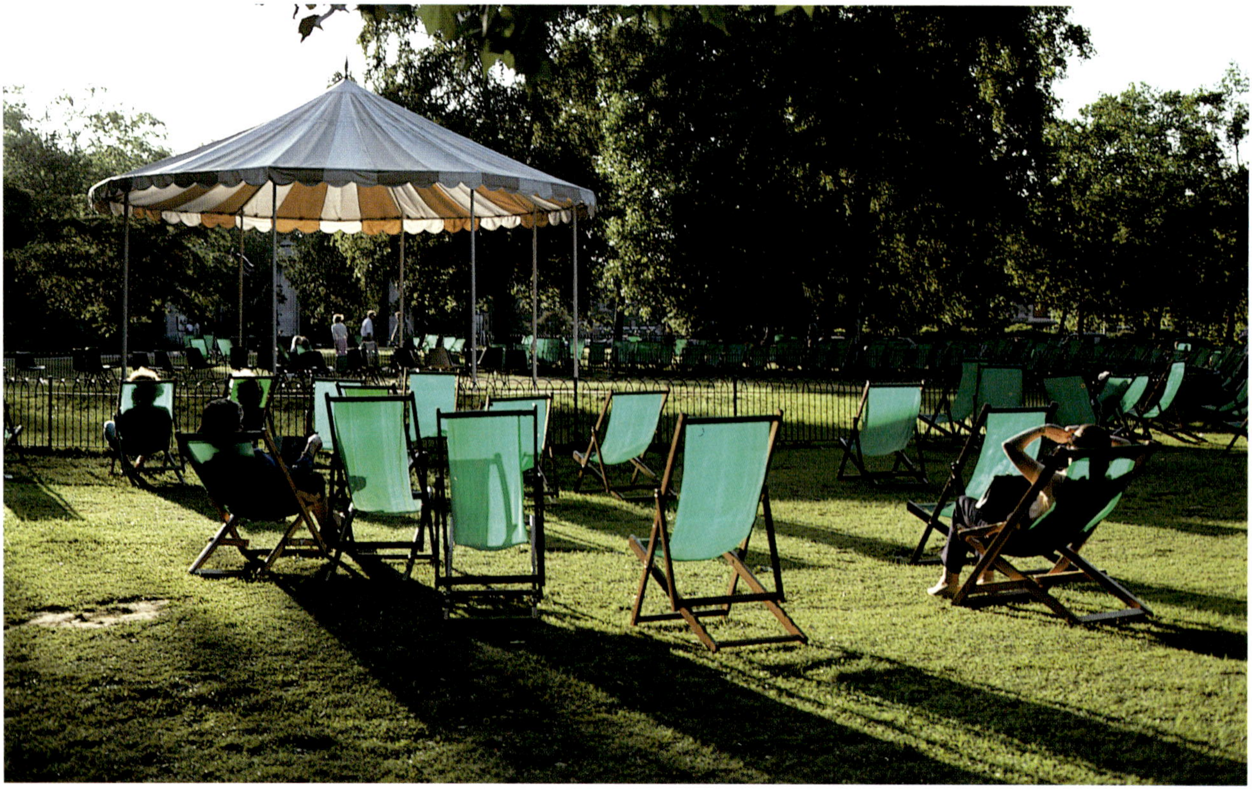

The Royal Botanic Gardens at Kew (*left*) are both a public park and a scientific institution. Its 300 acres/122 ha present a lavish vista of greenery, abundantly stocked with flowers and trees among which the Pagoda, the Temperate, Alpine, Australian and Palm Glasshouses, the Princess of Wales Conservatory, the Marianne North Gallery, Kew Palace and Queen Charlotte's Cottage offer something of interest all year round.

The Princess of Wales Conservatory (*inset left*) was opened in 1987. It is the newest, largest and most complex planthouse at Kew. The different climatic zones it recreates make it possible for a wide range of plants – from tropical to desert – to flourish.

Very central and very popular, St James's (*below left*) is the oldest royal park. Its particular attractions include live performances from the bandstand in summer, the collection of wildfowl on and around Duck Island, and the spectacular views from the bridge across the lake: Whitehall's domes and spires in one direction, Buckingham Palace in another.

Regent's Park (*below*) is a lasting memorial to George IV who, while Prince Regent, supported Nash's plans for its development in the early 19thC. Its 470 acres/122 ha, partially encircled by elegant Regency terraces, contain London Zoo, Queen Mary's Rose Garden, a boating lake, an open-air theatre and the Regent's Canal. There are plenty of places to walk or relax in a quiet spot.

The Yeoman Warders, popularly known as Beefeaters (*above*), were formed by Henry VII as his personal bodyguard. While their colourful Tudor uniform makes them appealing photographic subjects, they are also very entertaining tour guides. You can be sure they know where they are going because all 42 Beefeaters live, with their families, within the Tower of London precincts. Street entertainers (*right*) can be seen and heard in many parts of London, but you can always be sure of a good show in and around Covent Garden Piazza. The cheerful bustle of the old flower market provides an excellent backdrop for any entertainer.

Chelsea pensioners (*above*) live in the Royal Hospital where they are provided with board and lodging. Their colourful uniform, blue in winter and scarlet in summer with a three-cornered hat for special occasions, dates from the 18thC. Based on Louis XIV's Hôtel des Invalides in Paris, the Hospital was founded by Charles II in 1681 as a home for retired soldiers. His portrait hangs in the panelled hall of the North block.

If you're not part of it, the daily commuter rush from main-line stations to the City makes quite a spectacle, especially on London and Waterloo Bridges. Not such a familiar sight as he used to be, the traditionally-dressed British businessman (*right*), complete with bowler hat, can still be spotted.

Although it is such a large city, London still has identifiable 'villages' or communities. One of the liveliest is Soho in central London where the thriving Chinese community brings a distinctive flavour to the area. Gerrard Street (*left*) is generally acknowledged as the centre of Chinatown. It is a pedestrian precinct with ornate gateways at both ends, pagoda-shaped telephone boxes and street signs in Chinese. There are numerous Chinese restaurants, businesses and shops in the surrounding streets. A particularly good time to visit is on a Sunday when the Chinese families gather over dim sum (snacks) before an afternoon spent shopping and strolling. Another centre of activity in Soho is Berwick Street (*above*) which hosts a noisy and hectic market every day except Sunday. Principally known for its fruit and veg, the local residents and office workers, who throng the street at lunchtime, also come here for cheese, meat, fish and household goods.

NICHOLSON PHOTO GUIDE

LONDON

Each visitor to London has their own view of this great city: it is a historical and cultural capital; a financial centre; the home of British democratic government; the perfect backdrop to all the pomp and pageantry surrounding the British monarchy; the source of great institutions and great eccentrics; and a city where, despite the hectic pace of urban living, you are never far from an oasis of peace. This book shows London from many angles and will help you recall your own favourite image of this colourful and diverse capital.

CONTENTS

Trafalgar Square (*above left*) is one of London's most famous landmarks. Dominated by Nelson's Column, (145ft/44m high), people and pigeons flock here to see and enjoy the fountains, lions and many statues. The statue of Eros in the middle of Piccadilly Circus (*left*) is a popular meeting place – an area full of flashing neon.